LINCOLN

P9-DFW-100

Education Of Missionaries'
Children: The Neglected
Dimension Of World Mission

LINCOLN CHRISTIAN COLLEGE

Education Of Missionaries' Children: The Neglected Dimension Of World Mission

d. bruce lockerbie

William Carey Library

533 HERMOSA STREET • SOUTH PASADENA, CALIF. 91030

Copyright © 1975 by D. Bruce Lockerbie

All rights reserved.

No part of this book may be used or reproduced in any manner whatsoever without written permission, except in the case of brief quotations
embodied in critical articles and reviews.

In accord with some of the most recent thinking in the academic press, the William Carey Library is pleased to present
this scholarly book which has been prepared from an author-
edited and author-prepared camera-ready manuscript.

Library of Congress Cataloging in Publication Data

Lockerbie, D   Bruce.
    Education of missionaries' children.

    Includes bibliographical references.
    1. Children of missionaries--Education. I. Title.
LC5096.L62   377'.6   75-12726
ISBN 0-87808-422-3

Published by the William Carey Library
533 Hermosa Street
South Pasadena, Calif. 91030
Telephone 213-799-4559

PRINTED IN THE UNITED STATES OF AMERICA

CONTENTS

Preface

Strategy is the key word today in the enterprise called world mission. Men and women called of God to carry the Good News still respond to that call in courage sustained by prayer; but they no longer go as participants in a sanctified version of Blind Man's Buff. They no longer set out as crude pioneers to "discover" and colonize those to whom they will preach. Instead they are sent to areas often well known to cultural anthropologists, geological surveyors, and linguistic scientists.

The combined knowledges of these secular experts have contributed to the growing discipline called missiology-- the study of mission and its development historically, theologically, anthropologically, or pragmatically. Into this study have been enlisted the services of meteorology, medical research, agriculture, and demographic surveys. All are augmented by the wonders of data processing, storage, and retrieval. Together experts design strategies for world missionary evangelization in our time.

At the 1974 International Congress on World Evangelization held at Lausanne, Switzerland, one heard reports of strategies aimed at reaching the two billion yet-unreached peoples before this century ends. Most of these strategies call for some measure of cross-cultural evangelism: missionaries from one nation leaving home to live among people

in a foreign land, in obedience to the command of Jesus
Christ, to "go forth therefore and make all nations my
disciples" (Matthew 28:19, *New English Bible*).

Cross-cultural missionary service engages every aspect
of the missionary's life; it also affects his family, especially his children. The problems surrounding the missionary family are never easily solved, but neither will
they simply go away if the Church ignores them. Remarkably, in all the talk at Lausanne of strategy, no speaker
addressed the Congress on how to deal with the most emo-
tion-laden of these problems, the education of missionaries' children.

A tour of Asia and part of Africa took my wife Lory,
our three teenaged children, and me to more than a dozen
schools and to several more mission stations. This report
contains our observations and recommendations, many of
which are equally applicable to Christian schools in North
America.

We have seen marked evidence of earnestness and dedica-
tion among missionaries who serve as administrators and
teachers in these overseas schools. Yet overall the impression given--at Lausanne, at mission board headquar-
ters, at the level of the local church--is that education
of missionary dependents continues to be the neglected
dimension of world mission.

Our tour of mission schools was made possible by a sabbatical leave granted by The Stony Brook School and was
conducted under the official auspices of the Board of
Trustees of the School, Wilbert F. Newton, President, and
Dr. Donn M. Gaebelein, Headmaster.

In addition, financial support and other encouragement
from the following organizations and individuals is grate-
fully acknowledged:

Mr. and Mrs. Robert Bell, Stony Brook, New York
Mr. and Mrs. William Bridge, Stony Brook, New York
Clen-Moore United Presbyterian Church, New Castle, Penna.
Mr. and Mrs. Harry Duncan, Wheaton, Illinois
The Faculty of Fuller Theological Seminary School of World
   Mission, Pasadena, California, Dr. Arthur F. Glasser,
   Dean

Dr. Frank E. Gaebelein, Headmaster Emeritus, The Stony
   Brook School
Dr. and Mrs. Clarence Jones, Largo, Florida
Mrs. Jeanette W. Lockerbie, Pasadena, California
Mr. Ward Melville, Stony Brook, New York
Mount Sinai United Church of Christ, Mount Sinai, New York;
   the Reverend Robert Lee, Pastor
Mr. and Mrs. George Ogilvie, Brooklyn, New York
Tenth Presbyterian Church, Philadelphia, Pennsylvania; Dr.
   James M. Boice, Pastor
The Three Village Church, East Setauket, New York; the
   Reverend William L. O'Byrne, Pastor
Tyndale House Foundation, Wheaton, Illinois

   I also wish to thank several anonymous donors.

   Special thanks is offered to the administration and
faculty of each school who provided welcome and hospitality
during our visit; and to individuals and faculty at several
schools for their expressions of appreciation of our ministry among them.

1
Why? and Where?

For several years prior to the school year 1973-1974, my wife and I had been discussing how we might spend our impending sabbatical leave. Conversations with friends who had travelled abroad led us to consider volunteering to serve at a Christian school overseas. During seventeen years at Stony Brook, we had met students from many of the well-known schools for missionaries' children. But before we had made any inquiries into that possibility, a new direction for service presented itself.

Nebulous at first, this new thought began to suggest itself as an itinerant consultantship, travelling from school to school, sharing with administrators and teachers some of our experience at Stony Brook, a Christian college preparatory boarding school for boys and girls. In particular, we sought to provide encouragement to teachers within our own respective fields of teaching: My wife Lory is an elementary school nurse and teacher of health education; I have been chairman of the English department and also a teacher of Bible, coach, choir director, dormitory supervisor--the usual boarding school duties.

We first tested the idea with men whose counsel we had sought before: Dr. Frank E. Gaebelein, Headmaster Emeritus of The Stony Brook School, and Dr. Clarence Jones, former president of HCJB, "The Voice of the Andes." They encouraged us to carry the project further and sound out the heads of several schools abroad. This was the spring of 1972.

In September 1972, we sent a letter of introduction and a prospectus to 25 schools, offering to come for a period of not more than three weeks. We suggested that during the visit we might serve in some of the following ways: by presenting lecture-and-discussion opportunities in topics relating to Christian schooling; by teaching classes and consulting with teachers in our own disciplines; by conferring with college placement and testing counselors; by preaching in chapel worship services; or whatever other service might be valuable.

The terms of our plan were simple. The consultantship was being offered at no fee or honorarium whatsoever. In return we asked for ground transportation from the nearest airport, food and accommodations during the visit, and the opportunity for our three children to attend classes and otherwise participate in the life of the school. (At the proper point in this report, a statement regarding the contribution of our children to the success of the tour will be necessary; here it is sufficient to mention their names and ages: Don, then 16, Kevin, 15, and Ellyn, 13). The major financial burden, namely the air fare, we had already committed to the Lord to help us.

By January 1973, a flow of correspondence had begun between Stony Brook and the two dozen schools that had responded affirmatively to our offer. Eventually we had to interpret the exigencies of conflicting school calendars and travel schedules as guidance in arranging our itinerary, thereby eliminating certain schools whose invitation we should otherwise have accepted. We are particularly sorry to have missed visits to Faith Academy in The Philippines, Murree Christian School in Pakistan, and Ahlman Academy in Afghanistan.

Eventually the itinerary took shape around the following schools:

Christian Academy in Japan   Tokyo, Japan
(Grades 1-12) John
Jones, Headmaster

Osaka Christian School   Osaka, Japan
   (Grades 1-6) Richard
   Hazel, Principal

Morrison Academy (Grades 1-   Taichung, Taiwan
   12) Charles D. Holsinger,
   Superintendent

Bethany Christian School   Taipei, Taiwan
   (Grades 1-8) Frederick
   Wentz, Principal

Hong Kong Christian Schools   Hong Kong
   (Grades 1-12) William
   Decker, Superintendent

The Master's School (Grades   Bangkok, Thailand
   1-3) Michael Wynn, chair-
   man of Planning Committee

Dalat School (Grades 1-12)   Penang, Malaysia
   Carl G. Roseveare,
   Director

Chittagong Christian School   Chittagong, Bangladesh
   (Grades 1-6) Eugene
   Gurganus, Station Director

Hebron Christian School   Lama, Bangladesh
   (Grade 1) Willard
   Benedict, Station Director

Malumghat Christian School   Malumghat, Bangladesh
   (Grades 1-8) Mrs. Jesse
   Eaton, Station School
   Committee Chairman

Woodstock Academy (Grades   Mussoorie, India
   1-12) Robert Alter,
   Superintendent

Kodaikanal School (Grades   Kodaikanal, India
   1-12) Frank Jayasinghe,
   Principal

Rift Valley Academy (Grades   Kijabe, Kenya
   1-12) Herbert Downing,
   Principal

Bingham Academy (Grades   Addis Ababa, Ethiopia
   1-10) Donald Ricker,
   Acting Principal

Good Shepherd School   Addis Ababa, Ethiopia
   (Grades 1-12) Gilbert
   Anderson, Superintendent

The period of school visits extended from January 7
through April 21. I am astonished to discover that during
those weeks I spoke on more than 150 occasions, including
faculty meetings, board meetings, parents' meetings, chapel
and mission station services, and, not counting informal
coffee breaks or other social events that inevitably turned
into discussions of Christian schooling; I also taught more
than 50 classes. My wife made no record of her appointments, but in school after school she was engaged by elementary grade teachers, girls' physical education teachers,
and dormitory supervisors for teaching or dormitory devotions.

At certain schools our visit formed the basis for the
faculty's professional growth workshop, drawing the faculty
back to the school before the resumption of classes for a
new term. These were occasions for particularly intensive
discussion over several sessions and lasting several days.
At other schools, meetings were held during or after a
regular school day. At two schools our visit began without
plans for faculty meetings; these developed, however,
through natural acquaintanceships and a developing interest
in the reason for our presence.

At only a few schools was the faculty prepared for the
arrival of visiting consultants; even where information had
been provided in advance, it sometimes failed to allay
faculty fears that they were somehow about to be "evaluated"
by strangers. Unfortunate experiences with touring experts
in the past sometimes made our initial reception by individual teachers understandably cautious. It remained,
therefore, our responsibility to make our purposes manifest
by the nature of our presentations and conversations. We
had come to *share*, not to compare one school with another.

Such too must also be the spirit in which this report is read. Those looking for a detailed analysis of Christian schools, particularly those established for children of missionaries, must wait until such a report is written.[1] This report is not a decennial evaluation by a committee of the Middle States Association of Colleges and Secondary Schools; it does not attempt to rank one school against another.

A critical evaluation of Christian schooling, both at home and overseas, should be conducted. Until it is, we hope that the description of our findings can contribute to the further effectiveness of those who serve Christ through world mission and education.

2

Control and Administration

The fifteen schools we visited represent three kinds of
control: (1) single mission ownership; (2) multi-mission
cooperative ownership; (3) ownership by an independent
board of trustees, similar to the American "independent"
school.

(1) Single mission ownership:

Africa Inland Mission sponsoring Rift Valley Academy
Association of Baptists for World Evangelism sponsoring
    Chittagong, Hebron, and Malumghat Christian Schools
Christian and Missionary Alliance sponsoring Dalat School
Christian Missions in Many Lands sponsoring Hong Kong
    Christian Schools
Sudan Interior Mission sponsoring Bingham Academy

(2) The following mission societies sponsor one or more of
these schools:

American Baptist Foreign Mission Society
American Lutheran Church
American Mission (Presbyterian)
Assemblies of God
Baptist General Conference
Canadian Baptist Mission
Christian and Missionary Alliance
Christian Missionary Fellowship

Conservative Baptist Foreign Mission Society
Far Eastern Gospel Crusade
Lutheran Church in America
Lutheran Church--Missouri Synod
Mennonite Mission in Ethiopia .
Oriental Missionary Society
Overseas Missionary Fellowship
Reformed Church in America
Southern Baptist Church
The Evangelical Alliance Mission
United Church Board (United Church of Christ)
United Church of Canada
United Methodist Church
United Presbyterian Church

Bethany Christian School
Christian Academy in Japan
Good Shepherd School
Kodaikanal School
Morrison Academy
Osaka Christian School
Woodstock Academy

The third class of school, wholly independent, is represented by The Master's School in Bangkok, in the process
of organizing under a governing board consisting largely of
parents of intended pupils.

Both Woodstock Academy and Kodaikanal School, although
not in this class as of the time of our visit, were well
along in separate discussions leading to each school's independence of present sponsoring mission societies. This
move toward autonomy comes after each school had rejected a
recommendation by a joint committee that they merge.

Some mission societies, while not participating in ownership of a school, enter into agreement with a school
convenient to its areas of service to educate the children
of its missionaries. Such an agreement may either provide
for the use of the school's dormitory facilities and supervision, or else the mission society may supply boarding accommodations and supervision in a nearby hostel under its
own control.

Some schools are unhappy with either arrangement, although they recognize that enrolling children from outside

the single sponsoring mission may be considered advanta-
geous from the standpoint of breadth. In these schools
one hears a good deal of talk about "a home away from home"
and "the unity of the home." The metaphor supports the argument that, while society may be pluralistic, a home, a
family, is singular; the school-as-home needs to preserve
for its "family members"--the missionaries who constitute
the "family" on the grounds of expressed agreement with the
principles by which the mission society runs its school--an
environment free from any outside negative influences.

But the problem cannot simply be left there because in
many parts of the world, Christian mission societies must
rely upon the goodwill of those societies with schools to
admit children from societies without schools. The sponsoring missions, therefore, are constantly being asked to
allow the enrollment of children from other groups. Reluc-
tantly they comply, in most cases. Their reluctance sometimes shows itself in the stipulations made limiting full
participation in school life by children not within "the
family."

Not uncommonly the very problem of differing standards--
in education, discipline, or Christian practice--feared
from the outset by the controlling mission affects relationships among the several groups. A protest over some
form of restriction comes from an outside parent; immedi-
ately a defensive attitude toward the school's policies
conveys, by inference if not by direct statement, the
thought that the controlling mission must be on the alert
against attempts of outsiders to weaken the will of administrators and faculty. Particular attention seems drawn
toward dress, length of hair, preferences in music, and
alleged "bad attitudes" on the part of students from the
outside groups.

Solutions to this problem lean toward establishing
quotas in the future so that not more than a certain minority of students will be admitted from outside the controlling mission. The seriousness of such decisions can be
understood only if one also realizes that the solution may
require the school to contract in size, since the controlling mission's own number of families with student poten-
tial may be diminishing. In another instance the intensity
of feeling leads to the dismissal of a headmaster after
many years of service, the controlling board of education

feeling that his policies have failed to keep the school strictly enough in line with their wishes. This decision has been met with outspoken hostility from the majority of faculty and many students, particularly because the board's choice for a replacement is a missionary without academic training.

Happily, we can report, schools sponsored by several mission societies seem to have recognized their inherent problems initially and set about to meet them through open discussion and evidences of Christian moderation. To be sure, we do find instances in which the school yields over-much to some particular parent's narrowly sectarian opinion. For example, one parent would not allow his child to study the Bible in Mr. X's class: The school permitted that student to receive full credit for study with her father at home! But for the most part, we find a spirit of goodwill governing these schools.

Sponsoring mission societies, whether in sole ownership or cooperation, usually provide liaison between the school's administration and the home office through an education committee or individual officer of the society. In most cases these committees or education secretaries are situated in the United States and make only occasional field trips. To provide "local" control, most societies establish a school board consisting of missionaries--parents of present students, for the most part--with whom administrators and faculty, as well as other parents and non-parent missionaries, may consult.

"Local" may, however, be a misleading term, for all the sponsoring society's good intentions. Members of the school board may, in fact, live at distances too great to allow easy communication with the school and its problems. This will be true especially if it is the society's policy to have each of its stations or areas of service represented on the board. Conversely, "local" may become "localized" if the board, for reasons of facilitating communication, draws its members from a narrowly regional base of proximity to the school.

Administrative structure and day-by-day control of schools differ widely from one institution to another, and this fact is not necessarily correlated with either single-

or multi-mission sponsorship. Except where schools are op-
erated as an adjunct to the office of the station director
or his appointed committee, each school has a chief administrator variously known as headmaster, principal, superintendent, or director. I shall use the term *headmaster*
throughout for generic simplicity and to differentiate
"head of school" from that subordinate position which in
some schools is also called "principal."

In most cases the headmaster fulfills responsibilities
important to the existence of any foreign enterprise in an
alien country, but these are not uniquely educational. He
must be well versed in national law and customs; he will
often participate in local government functions; he may
maintain a special relationship with various United States'
consular or military personnel. He will be a part-time
diplomat, and he may find his responsibilities made doubly
onerous because of the petty bureaucracy and frequently
blatant requests for graft and bribery from national offi-
cials.

In all but the smallest schools we found the headmaster
to be somewhat removed from immediate contact with students
--indeed, in some instances, with faculty--and concentrat-
ing his efforts upon public relations, faculty or student
recruitment, fund raising, mission policies beyond the
limits of school administration, or supervision of the
national employees. More customary matters of school administration such as curriculum development, faculty responsibilities, school calendar and scheduling, problems
related to dormitory life, counseling and discipline, and
the maintenance of Christian worship and service opportunities are generally in the hands of assistants--academic
coordinators or grade-level principals, residential supervisers, school pastors or chaplains. Conversations with
students and faculty often revealed a fundamental unfamil-
iarity with the headmaster and, not surprisingly, sometimes
a concomitant mistrust. This situation is ameliorated,
however, in the two schools where the headmaster coaches a
varsity team.

Subordinate administrators, whatever their titles, in
general appear to have much more frequent and broad contact with students and faculty. Some may teach a class or
coach a team; some live with their families in dormitory

apartments and may eat their meals in the school's dining room--on which point a later comment will be made.

In most situations we found that, for all practical purposes, the school was under the governance of an administrative assistant. Planning and programming of our visit were often under his direction, with the headmaster taking a retiring role; in some instances, the headmaster attended only one or two of our meetings.

A notable difference between headmasters and their assistants is in length of service. Several headmasters have spent fifteen-to-twenty years; one more than forty. Their assistants, however, are often on short-term contracts of three or four years, either with a mission society or with the school itself. The resultant turn-over in personnel is high. At the administrative level such a policy appears to undermine stability.

In our opinion, a factor determining the effectiveness of administrative assistants in particular (although this also applies to faculty) derives from their background and professional experience. They are almost uniformly educated in the American public schools; their previous experiences as classroom teachers and administrators has been almost exclusively in the public school system. They now find themselves responsible, however, for administering a *Christian* school; not only so, but in many instances a *boarding* school as well. Yet they are without prior acquaintance at first hand with either or both types of institution--although not always without negative attitudes towards the Christian boarding school.

Not being familiar with the American boarding school, they lack a sense of its advantages, able as it is to offer a residential education in whatever environment for learning it wishes to create. Not being familiar with a reputable Christian school and not having articulated for themselves an evangelical philosophy of Christian schooling,[2] they come to their positions without knowing the opportunities to provide education that is both whole and wholly Christian.

Together these twin liabilities call into question the very tradition of which their present schools are a part-- the tradition of the Christian boarding school, first es-

tablished by Vittorino da Feltre in 1423 for the purpose of
removing children from the grip of secularism during their
formative years and placing them in a milieu conducive to
Christian nurture. Consequently, the function of this
school may be regarded merely as satisfying an unfortunate
necessity brought about by the peculiar demands of the missionary vocation.

The Christian boarding school overseas is seldom regarded by members of its own administration and faculty as
good in and of itself. Time after time we were asked the
question, "We know why parents send their children here--
they *have* to! But why would anybody want to send a child
away from an American public school to a school like Stony
Brook?"

Only once did we find a response from a faculty member
of the host school, a woman who pointed out that (1) it is
a sentimentalism to consider missionary children deprived
by having to accept a boarding education; (2) literally
thousands of American families scrimp and save (as her
family had done) to be able to afford to send their children to just such a school in Pennsylvania; and (3) she is
tired of apologizing to colleagues, parents, and students
for the type of education deemed desirable by outsiders!

Other happy exceptions, although none as outspoken, were
the several alumni of missionary schools whom we found having returned as teachers expressly because they recognize
the importance of the education they had themselves received. Whether their enthusiasm extends in every case to
Christian schooling at home as well as abroad, we are unable to judge.

3

Faculty and Staff

We were privileged to meet many people in these schools
to whom we offer the highest personal praise by saying: We
wish they were among our colleagues at Stony Brook. Many
of these men and women are well educated, personally disciplined to scholarship, effective teachers, good examples
to growing young people of vital Christian faith in action.

Having so said, two observations are necessary before
continuing this section:

(1) We rarely heard the word *faculty* used to denote members
of the teaching profession, missionaries who had responded
to the Christian vocation of teaching. Instead, they were
"the staff."

(2) We found that most of the boarding schools were unfa-
miliar with the standard American practice in boarding
schools, that of building unity around the faculty member
who both teaches and supervises a dormitory residence. Instead, most of these schools have dual hiring of classroom
teachers and so-called "dorm parents."

Each of these observations has implications far more
serious than any superficial differences in semantics or
structure. Indeed, they are closely related in the sense
that language connotes attitudes. In certain specific instances it is clear that the school does not know the dis-

tinctions between *faculty*--suggesting scholarship and
learning--and *staff*--a word perfectly suitable to the dignity of labor but applicable to persons trained, not educated. Likewise where the term "dorm parents" is used to
signify a special class of person in a boarding school, the
very categorization of responsibilities alters the delicate
balance of relationships within a context of *in loco paren-
tis*, "the parents of the locale."

Dormitory specialists are necessary to care for younger
children, in grades 1-6, perhaps; but observation of these
schools confirms what experience at our own has shown us:
that adolescent boys and girls are capable of living together in harmony and increasing maturity within a boarding
school environment without the fulltime presence of surrogate parents. Furthermore, we observe that the setting up
of authority figures--in addition to natural parents and
teachers--in the lives of adolescents just beginning to
test their own independence can lead to frequent and sometimes volatile clashes of will among superfluous adults and
their charges.

Discussion of the rationale behind the divided faculty/
staff reveals an alarming--not to mention insulting--esti-
mate of faculty integrity. The claim is made, by more than
one headmaster, that, in the first place, obtaining qualified teachers is difficult enough; it would be nearly impossible if to their other duties were added the task of
living with students. In the second place, parents doubt
the capacity of most teachers--presumably Christian, adult,
professional--to treat fairly those dormitory residents who
are also in their classes. The child who misbehaves in a
dormitory--so the fear goes--will not be given a fair deal
in the classroom, if the same person is responsible for him
in both settings.

Our disagreement with the first clause is confirmed by
what we know of schools whose faculty are serving as both
teachers and resident supervisers. Our outrage at the
second clause compels silence.

Problems in hiring tax every school administrator. For
the overseas headmaster they are often baffling to the
point of grimness. Some schools now provide funds for an
annual cross-country tour of the United States and Canada
during which the headmaster meets and interviews candidates

already passed through previous screenings by the home office. But these tours are brief, exhausting, and demand a
hasty judgment of character that sometimes misses the mark.
Other schools conduct all the hiring through the home office with the headmaster specifying his needs and the mission board doing its best to match candidates to fill those
needs.

Sometimes both teacher and school discover upon his arrival that his assignment exceeds or even ignores his academic preparation and qualifications to teach. Communication lapses, misunderstandings between parties, or the occasional unethical tactic by an enthusiastic mission execu-
tive--a slap on the back and the dare, "Hey, you can teach
that to junior high kids, can't you?"--these complications
disrupt the teacher's period of adjustment and may render
him ineffective throughout his term of service.

To satisfy the immediate need for teachers, most sponsoring missions resort to short-term appointments.[3] On the
surface the program seems attractive for obvious reasons
both to candidates and to mission societies. Yet it is not
satisfactory educational planning. The constant turn-over
in teachers means an added measure of instability to the
school community. The fact that most short-termers are
young people in the early years of their professional experience often limits the bulk of the faculty to novices.
While most short-termers are sincere about their present
commitment, a minority still seems to possess what one
headmaster calls "the Peace Corps attitude" that resigns
itself to any kind of job in exchange for foreign travel.
Of course, some short-term appointees return as fully accepted missionary teachers, but their number is few.

One school faced the prospect of 26 teachers departing
at the end of the 1973-74 school year; the majority of
these were short-termers whose contracts have expired. We
find it difficult to suppose that turn-over of this kind
can be beneficial to a school's growth and improvement.

In order to be a *school*, an institution must provide its
teachers, as well as its students, with opportunities to go
on learning. Several factors mitigate against the fulfillment of this requirement in most mission schools; hence,
these deterrents conspire to reduce faculty to being day-
laborers.

First, most teachers carry inordinate classroom responsibilities, both in number of daily class meetings but also
(and more taxing) in different preparations. We became
acquainted with teachers, for example, whose daily work
load consisted of the following:

Miss F
Coordination of English instruction throughout the school
English 9
English 10
English 11-12 (1st elective)
English 11-12 (2nd elective)
English 11-12 (3rd elective)
Journalism
Year book
Direction of the school play, then in rehearsal

Mr. P
Social Studies 7
Social Studies 8
English 9
English 10
Bible 9
Bible 10

Mr. F
English 12
Bible 12
Psychology (two large classes)
United States' History
Direction and daily rehearsal of 60-voice school choir
Coach of varsity rugby

Each of these persons, along with others we met, is an
unusually energetic person, the type who thrives on activ-
ity. But even granting that asset, one must question how
long any teacher can reasonably be expected to maintain a
high level of day-to-day preparation in four, five, or six
different reading courses, while also performing other
duties and conducting any sort of personal life.

Having offered these examples of overloaded teachers, it
may seem contradictory to cite as a second limiting factor
to a school's effectiveness the severed contacts of
teachers with boarding school students after class hours.
Certainly hard-working adults and hard-working students

need relief from work and often from each other. But in
the boarding situation, as we observe it, one cannot redeem
a former liability by a latter necessity.

The fabric of a boarding school depends upon the establishing and maintaining of a sense of wholeness in faculty-
student relationships. In schools where all or most of the
faculty live away from their students--often in rented
housing far superior to dormitory residents' accommodations
--we have seen fewer instances of this wholeness. These
teachers arrive in time for classes and leave at the end of
the academic schedule, much like public day school teachers.
They eat their meals separately; they are, in general, acquainted with their students only in the classroom.

Their counterparts, the "dorm parents," pick up their
duties at the end of classes--Note that we do not say "at
the end of *school*," for in a boarding school, presumably,
learning should never terminate with the ringing of a
class-change bell. The husband or wife, or in some cases
the single woman or widow, greets the returning children at
the dormitory. Afternoon refreshments may be served.
Playtime may be supervised. In some cases the day's laun-
dry, freshly washed and ironed by the dorm mother or a
national worker, may be distributed. The evening meal,
study supervision, and bedtime devotions are the responsibility of the dorm parents. Prompt rising and breakfast,
followed at a few schools by elementary chores before
classes, complete the cycle. When the students go off to
class, the dorm parents' clerical duties begin: writing
letters to parents, tabulating allowances, collecting the
daily or weekly wash, conferring with one another on prob-
lems--in most instances, rarely receiving time away from
the campus for more than a couple of hours at a time, pos-
sibly as seldom as once every ten days.

In other words, from what we can observe in these boarding schools, most of the students' dealings with adults
must be divided between those who teach them and those with
whom they live. Furthermore, all too often there appears
to be little or no communication between teachers and dorm
parents. When we learned that at one school dormitory personnel had not yet had relief from evening supervision
since the beginning of the year, we asked about teachers'
providing that relief. One teacher replied, "I'll take his

duty when one of those dorm parents offers to teach my
classes." In school after school we found similar divi-
sions.

Nor are these tensions disguised from students. That
favorite trick of schoolboys, setting up one adult against
another with two versions of the same story, is easily
practised in this situation. Especially is this true when
teachers and dorm parents rarely meet for conferences; when
dorm parents learn of a resident's academic difficulties
through the student grapevine, or when teachers learn of a
student's dormitory difficulties only in the same manner.

Unquestionably the factor weighing most heavily upon
some faculty is the burden of extra-educational mission
responsibilities which so many understand to be expected of
them. To be sure, these expectations may be more assumed
than real; only in rare instances can we report actual
assignments beyond normal boarding school duties.

Such an exception deserves mention, however, because it
illustrates the disregard in which missionary colleagues
hold teachers at one school. Mission policy allows an annual four-week vacation. The mission school has three
four-week vacations separating terms. At this particular
school the overload upon teachers is severe, and unlike the
majority of schools, most dormitory supervisers here are
also fulltime teachers. This means that, quite apart from
needing emotional release from the constancy of their work,
they also need the so-called vacation time for class pre-
paration--a luxury hardly available during the school term
itself. Yet the sponsoring mission, in apparent response
to complaints that faculty were receiving too much vacation
time, has instituted a mandatory work program whereby each
faculty member must sign up to perform certain manual or
clerical work during each interim when school is not in
session.

Usually, such pressures as exist spring not from the institution but from within the faculty member himself or
from his sponsoring churches. There exists in the mentality of the American church a fixed idea of what constitutes
mission service--trekking into the jungle, confronting
witch doctors and cannibals, living in a mud hut with a
thatched roof. The missionary teacher arrives "on the
field" and discovers that his work center may be a modern

biology lab or a social studies classroom equipped with
maps and audio-visual aids or a gymnasium complex; there he
will instruct young people in science, history, or physical
education. "Can this be missionary service?" he asks.

Until he finds assurance in the fulfillment of his
Christian vocation, the missionary teacher may struggle for
some additional means to justify his being there--conduc-
ting a Bible study for nationals, attempting village evangelism, experimenting in "church planting"--often to the
detriment of his primary responsibilities as a teacher.

Yet many teachers and some administrators confide the
fact that without reports of their extra-educational activities to include in their periodic letters, they would be
hardpressed to maintain the interest of supporters at home.
The scandalous truth is that we have met missionary educators who are even now facing the termination of support by
a church that no longer feels its money should go to some-
one whose phase of mission service fails to suit the mold.
Interestingly, we met no one among the "dorm parents" who
had been threatened with the cutting off of support. Ap-
parently their work serves to justify itself, whereas the
teaching of language and literature, mathematics and
science, does not.

But if the turn-over in teachers is critical, the appar-
ently greater turn-over among dormitory supervisers is
crippling. We met no full-time dorm parents who had served
more than five years; by far the majority are short term
appointees, young couples completing their first or second
year.[4] Some of these are appointees awaiting visas to a
different country; they have no calling to their present
position, and are merely marking time. According to the
testimony of our sons who lived in dormitories in eight
schools, some of these dorm parents are highly effective in
dealing with teenagers; others seem obviously unsuited by
temperament to the peculiar rigors of communal living and
its demands for judicious disciplining of other people's
children.

Here we must raise the knotty issue of qualifications
for dorm parents. Academic credentials can be misleading,
but at least they suggest areas in which a candidate may or
may not be qualified. But how does one evaluate the poten-

tial of a newly married couple, a middleaged early-retired
couple, a widow, or a bachelor, to deal with the daily
problems of boarding school life? No headmaster seems to
know the answer, but several agree that one of the telling
measurements for a mature couple ought to be their success
or failure in rearing their own children. But mission
societies seem reluctant to pry into such matters; in con-
sequence, some sadly incompetent adults--earnest but unwise,
inflexible, or vaccilating--arrive at a distant school to
repeat their parental follies.

Fortunately they are the minority. Yet few even among
the competent dorm parents express any interest in renewing
their contracts, and many speak of their disillusionment
with their terms of service, with the idea of a "Christian
school," or with the missionary enterprise in general.
Some heed should be paid to these grievances, particularly
to the inability of most schools to establish patterns of
shared duties among all faculty and staff. Other complaints also merit mentioning, if only to prompt mission
executives to re-examine specific policies.

It continues to seem incongruous to us that the written
policy of several mission societies is to *charge* dormitory
personnel for room and board. Surely if their presence is
considered necessary to the welfare of the students, then
the accommodations they occupy and the food they eat while
performing their duties ought to be perquisites of the position. To do otherwise violates, in our opinion, the
Scriptural teaching that a workman is worthy of his hire.

We also do not understand the policy requiring school-
aged children of dorm parents to leave their family quar-
ters and take up residence in their age-group dormitory.
Where this policy is in force, it purports to maintain
"fairness" so that students away from their parents will
not be offended by the natural child's living with his parents. Quite apart from the questionable sociology of this
reasoning, there is the matter of exemplary models to be
established and maintained. If, as these schools claim,
they intend to be "a home away from home," the nearest
model for *home* will be the natural home that students,
first, see in the dorm parents' relationships with their
own children and, next, appropriate to themselves as members of the extended dormitory "family."

Where faculty is separate from dorm parents, we can report little in the way of faculty entertaining. At one such school, we asked a mature 12th grade girl how often she visited the off-campus homes of faculty. When she looked puzzled by our question, we attempted to clarify, and she replied, "Oh, we're never invited there. The dorm parents do all our party-giving."

At most schools responsibility for entertaining the bulk of the students--at weekly socials, for special celebrations, or on an informal knock-and-enter basis--falls on the dormitory personnel. This burden is not only emotional but also financial. Dorm parents are expected to provide refreshments out of their own meager allowances. We know of no budgetary program taking this expense into consideration, and we met several dormitory couples whose regular hospitality has had to be curtailed because inflation has made their continued entertaining impossible.

The task of the dorm parent is taxing, ill-defined, and even where necessary sometimes unappreciated. But where it appears to be superfluous, the dorm parent is frequently of second-class importance. Not qualified to teach (as is often the case), he finds himself voiceless in an academic community. Not the true parent, he finds himself cast in the role of surrogate. In certain extreme instances, we heard the customary mission field designations for any adult, "Uncle" and "Auntie," confused with "Daddy" and "Mommy." Where an indulgent mission or school policy has pampered its students, dorm parents are reduced to valets or ladies-in-waiting, running errands, picking up dirty socks, to the amused contempt of students.

We observe that the best dormitory relationships obtain where most resident supervisors are fundamentally teachers whose homes happen to be in the dormitories, and there they share their lives with students.

We recall only a half-dozen or so national teachers, indicating how North American the faculties of these schools remain. Various reasons are given: lack of applicants, lack of candidates, inherent differences in the national teacher's methods of teaching and learning, problems in student respect for nationals, inadequacy of mission school salary to meet national scales--an interesting commentary on missionary stipends! Some schools, it is true,

use nationals in residential supervisory roles. At most
schools, however, the only nationals seen daily by students
are the coolies, peons, bearers, sweepers, and other
lackeys in menial positions. The happy exceptions are
schools in which nationals hold at least accounting or
other business managerial responsibilities.

4

Constituency

Ralph E. Bressler, Coordinator of Instruction at Dalat
School, has ennumerated, in two serial articles, the op-
tions in education available to foreign missionaries and
their children.[5] They are: (1) parental tutoring (usually
the mother's task) through established correspondence
courses such as the Calvert system, thereby keeping the
family together in the foreign country; (2) enrolling the
child, if possible, in the national system of education, if
any, which also allows the family to remain in the country;
(3) sending the child to a school for missionary children
in proximity to the family, thereby allowing some family
contact during the year; (4) sending the child to a public
or private school in the home country, thereby requiring
extended separations from family; (5) returning with the
child to the home country and remaining there until his
secondary schooling is completed before resuming foreign
service.

Of these, by far the most satisfactory is the third
option, and the schools on our itinerary are, with few exceptions, primarily schools for the children of missionaries. To deal with the exceptions first: The Hong Kong
Christian Schools, in which more than 6,000 children are
enrolled, serve the Chinese populace, particularly those
in the vast housing estates, with "rooftop schools." Here
the teaching is almost wholly in Chinese.

The Master's School intends to draw from the some-50,000
Anglo-Americans in Bangkok, representing missionary, business, embassy, and military families.

Although both Woodstock Academy and Kodaikanal School
were founded as schools for missionary children, their new
purposes identify them, respectively, as "a Christian international school"6 and as "an autonomous, plural-cultural,
multinational, Christian school in mission as a Christian
service to children and parents of all communities of
Indian and international society."7

Among the rest, Morrison Academy has held a unique position as the one school designated by the United States Department of Defense as an official school for children of
military personrel. Until the major withdrawal of American
forces from Taiwan in the fall of 1973, Morrison had
counted on its contract with the military bases nearby for
a substantial number of its total enrollment. This figure
will now be cut drastically.

Historically, as we indicate, most of these schools have
been primarily intended to educate children of Christian
missionaries. The degree to which they have been neglected,
however, in the scholarship and published discussion of
world mission may be noted by the fact that one reads
through many histories, biographies, or studies in missiology without finding so much as a passing reference to the
founding and maintaining of schools for the children of
those called to carry the Gospel to foreign lands.[8] It is
not difficult to acquire an impression that some mission
boards wish celibacy were practised by Protestant missionaries. Yet we do not even hear of these schools spoken of
as a *problem* that somehow must be dealt with; we do not
hear them spoken of at all! Underlying our initial impulse
to make this tour was the fact that, in thirty years of
active missionary interest--as a child I had made the cir-
cuit of major missionary conferences; I knew Oswald J.
Smith's slogan, "If God calls you to be a missionary, don't
stoop to be a king"; my parents had been home missionaries,
then deputizers for leprosy missions; my sister is a missionary in Bangladesh--in all those years *I have never once
heard* a public presentation of the ministry in mission that
is the missionary children's school.

65936

But if these schools and their problems have remained in
the background heretofore, it is unlikely that they can remain unnoticed in the near future. Most of the schools
that set out to educate only the children of mission personnel have broadened their constituency in recent years,
either voluntarily or under governmental pressures. Only
four schools--three controlled by a single mission in
Bangladesh and one cooperative school in Japan--restrict
themselves at present to missionaries' children. The
others all have either national, diplomatic, business, or
military families included in their constituencies. This
broadening within is bound to lead to greater exposure
without.

Beyond question these schools are benefiting from enrolling nationals, some of whom come from prestigious families
--grandchildren of the former Ethiopian emperor Haile
Selassie, children of cabinet ministers in Kenya, children
of ambassadors to Japan, Taiwan, India and Ethiopia. In
some cases the school has anticipated or responded to inti-
mations of quota-setting for enrollment of nationals by
local ministries of education; in other cases, the school
has welcomed nationals quite as a matter of course.

But for some schools the larger issue looms: Having
opened admissions to one group of non-missionary families,
should they next begin enrolling children from other non-
missionary families, particularly from the Anglo-American
community so often clamoring for admission. This urgency
is especially obvious among American families dissatisfied
with the often laissez-faire attitudes toward discipline
and learning found at American government-sponsored
schools.[9] According to administrators, teachers, and
students at representative American schools in Tokyo,
Taipei, Hong Kong, Bangkok, New Delhi, Nairobi, and Addis
Ababa, problems of a nature scarcely known to the Christian
school are endemic in a system largely characterized by
frequent administrative and faculty changes, constant tran-
sience of families, and the schools' inability to frame a
satisfactory ethical basis for education in a secular environment.

At this point, not unexpectedly, some of the tensions
already discussed on pages 7-9, with regard to the admission of outsiders, manifest themselves. Some missionary
parents are outspoken in demanding that their children be

shielded from association with children from non-missionary
families--a further development from the isolationism that
separates children of one mission board or denomination
from all others. Obviously these parents view schooling--
and in particular, Christian schooling--as *protection*
rather than *preparation*. Strangely enough, from none of
these worried parents, alarmed that their children might be
infected by unbelievers, did we hear mention of the possibility that their children might witness to and evangelize
the unbelievers.

A cultural parallel to this spiritual separation can be
seen in schools where European mission societies, wishing
to maintain among their children national customs and
language, have established hostels. In theory, these hostels ought to work in a cooperative relationship with the
school-at-large. European houseparents ought to strive to
guarantee a measure of continuity with both the national
culture and the children's present English-speaking education. The school too has its part: It ought to make provi-
sion for European students to receive instruction in their
native language, history, political science, and geography,
in place of standard North American studies. The school
ought to encourage European students to speak their native
language, to celebrate national festivals, to wear national
costumes.

At two schools we must report contrasting situations developing from their European hostels. The first school has
hired a German teacher who teaches throughout the secondary
school; she also lives with and instructs the German children in their hostel. We know from first hand observation
how well integrated these children are in the life of their
school, yet how unselfconsciously they speak and dress as
Germans. At another school, however, a group of children
in a Finnish hostel appear to be subject to a xenophobic
houseparent who has made derogatory remarks to the children
about the American school they attend, the English language
in which they are being instructed, and their English-
speaking teachers.

Clearly the responsibility for designing an appropriate
relationship between national and international interests
in a Christian school must rest with administrators and
mission board executives who recognize, beyond chauvinism,
the importance of the personal dimension of every child.

5

Students

Our dealings with students confirms a growing distaste
for the solecism terming them as "MK's"--missionary kids--
and their schools as "MK schools."[10] The sheer cuteness of
the terms is not itself at issue; cuteness in usage dis-
charges only upon the speaker himself. Rather, it is the
mentality, the attitude, associated with such usage that
is at fault, a mentality that readily lumps together individual persons and makes them into mere "MK's"--packaged
entities presumably typed, classified, and catalogued.
Because it ignores the person and looks instead at the
supposed class, usage of this kind may be convenient but
unChristian. We reject the term altogether.

We can describe the largest number of students we met by
a single, unscientific word: *normal*. By this we mean that
they appear to us to be healthy, well adjusted to their
school circumstances, interested in ideas of the worldwide
youth subculture, largely unconcerned by their present
alien status, yet eager to identify with their North American or European heritage.[11] A surprisingly small minority
contends that their parents' vocation has "cost" them any-
thing in loss of material comforts or future opportunities;
in almost every such case, the embittered student is a
teenager whose parents have only recently become missionaries, uprooting the family and moving out of familiar sur-
roundings just at the teenager's most difficult years.

At this point, we believe, it is appropriate to speak of the role that our own children took in this tour of schools. Wherever we visited a school in session with classes at their grade levels, Don (grade 11), Kevin (grade 9), and Ellyn (grade 8) were enrolled in a full academic program; in this way they were able to obtain credit for their studies from The Stony Brook School.

As full-time students engaged in the daily round of classes, meals, worship, athletics, extra-curricular clubs and social activities, our children saw these schools from a vantage we could never have obtained. As indicated earlier, our sons enjoyed the added experience of dormitory life in several schools. The relevance to this report of our children's intimate associations lies in the fact that through their acquaintanceships--indeed, friendships--with classmates and roommates, we came to know many individual students far better than we might have otherwise.

Many of them are personable and pleasant, eager to help visitors adjust to the new situation, eager to have us share with them their delight in the adopted country. We cannot report, however, that these students as a whole are scholastically as productive as we had expected.

If the findings of research such as Christopher Jencks' *Inequality*[12] are to be believed, the level of performance by students in these schools ought to be above the expectations of any but the most selective American independent schools. Parents of these children are educated well beyond national norms; many are skilled professionals, even world-renowned in their fields. Their children have been exposed to home environments in which the intellect yielded in service to God is a respected gift. These same children have known the advantages of travel and of living in different cultures. In some cases these benefits appear to have resulted in maturity and a freedom from parochial thinking.

In far too many instances, however, the desired results do not yet appear. We find that, on the whole, students at these schools exhibit tendencies toward ready acceptance of narrowly received opinions; they are largely underinformed concerning current events; if aroused to interest, they lack sufficient resources to develop that interest into enlightened criticism (See comments under *Curriculum* regard-

ing school deficiencies in library acquisitioning of periodicals). Perhaps most alarming is the apparent acquies-
cence of students to indoctrination under authoritarianism.
From first-hand observation in the classrooms we can de-
clare, the more authoritarian the school, the more re-
pressed is student response, even to inquiry or statements
intended to prod them into free expression.

Causes and consequences of this intellectual depression
require far more than a superficial gloss; we are not qualified to diagnose. We can say, however, that both our
children's comments and our own observations confirm that
the best classroom learning situations are those avoiding
indoctrination and mere "training"; rather, by seeking
through inquiry, induction, or Socratic dialogue to draw
students into the confidence of a teacher. It helps if
that teacher is not afraid to be confronted by a fresh idea
or by a question to which he has no easy reply. Unfortunately, we find such instances only rarely and, in some
schools, scarcely at all.

In short, although we can testify that each school has
its brilliant students, we find the general range of ac-
complishment to be less than might reasonably be expected,
and considerably below the laudatory self-assessments of
some administrators and faculty. Perhaps lacking the broad
perspective of larger student populations or failing to see
their students in competition with others, through testing
programs such as the Advanced Placement Program,[13] some
educators obtain an inflated estimate of their pupils'
abilities. Ultimately it is these pupils who suffer when
cold reality strikes them in college.

These schools, at least in their secondary grades, are
college preparatory; most students are college-bound. But
not all of them. Between ten and fifteen per cent of the
graduating class (even a greater number in some schools)
have no plan to attend college. In small schools such as
these, the two-track system of teaching is hardly feasible;
even if it were from a standpoint of faculty numbers, the
social implications of having a small student body classified by academic ability into multiple groupings might be
divisive. Hence a major student problem facing these
schools: What to do with the child whose minimal competence
disqualifies him from college preparation? Beyond this
problem lurk the even greater questions of how to deal with

brain damaged children, hyperkinetic children, children
suffering from dyslexia or other learning disabilities.

In addressing themselves to the former problem, most
schools seem to attempt to accommodate the non-academic
child in college preparatory courses where necessary, with
individual teachers responsible for adjusting assignments
and grades. His curriculum will be supplemented by courses
in auto mechanics, industrial arts, and perhaps home economics for boys; hopefully, he may also take an interest in
music or sports to round off his day. Yet the bulk of his
time is spent in academically oriented classes where even
under the most fairminded teacher such a child can hardly
avoid the bottom of the scale. The almost inevitable result is that by the time the child grows into late adolescence, he has acquired a self-image of personal failure
only because he has seldom, if ever, been placed in a
class of equal ability.

In the latter instances of dealing with emotional and
physical problems, two schools we visited are making deter-
mined efforts through ungraded elementary classes to bring
small groups of children into scholastic alignment with
their peers. One school, unusually well equipped with
audio-visual aids and learning apparatus, has been able to
offer individualized attention to its most needy students.
But this we find to be highly unusual. For the most part,
children in academic disadvantage must learn to struggle
along under whatever burdens of shame and inadequacy they
feel, bolstered by whatever motivations of pride they can
muster. The schools simply are not supplied with sufficient faculty to give them the attention they need.

The Lockerbie family in Hong Kong: (left to right)
Kevin, Ellyn, Bruce, Lory, and Don

The Main Buildings of Woodstock School, Mussoorie, North India

Bruce Lockerbie Addressing Students and Faculty at an Informal Worship Service at Kodaikanal School, South India

The Entrance to Bingham Academy, Addis Ababa, Ethiopia

6

Curriculum

With the obvious exception of the Hong Kong schools, all others on our tour follow an American curriculum. Elementary classes are self-contained; if available, specialists augment the classroom teacher's instruction. In small schools several grade levels may be represented in a single classroom, with part of the daily teaching being carried on as ungraded instruction. From grade seven on, courses are departmentalized, and distributive requirements for graduation ("Carnegie units") begin in grade nine.

A standard college preparatory curriculum found in typical American high schools (English, mathematics, sciences, social studies, foreign languages, and physical education) pertains also in these schools; in addition, students study the Bible. Few academic electives can be offered because of an already burdened faculty, although we do know that three schools are providing electives in English and social studies and others are wrestling with the problem. We recall no opportunities for guided independent study.

Offerings in foreign languages are generally weak, and some schools do not even offer instruction in the national language. Tied to this observation is the fact that few schools offer courses or even phases of instruction in the local geography, history, or culture.[14]

Health education, including preventive instruction in physical, mental, and social health problems (venereal disease, drug abuse, alcoholism), is rare. Most school nurses are not qualified teachers and so are restricted to clinical and first-aid responsibilities.

Home economics' kitchens, industrial arts and auto mechanics' workshops, and typing classrooms, well equipped with modern appliances and machines, testify to the schools' concern for excellence in these areas of instruction.

Most impressive to us are the programs in music--classroom, performing ensembles, and private study. Some schools have as many as 60% of their students receiving piano lessons, for instance. Several schools are equipped with music teaching and rehearsal facilities to rival colleges ten times their size. The quality of choral and instrumental performance confirms the value of this investment. In some cases a school's music program offers the European community its best opportunities for enjoying Western music. In at least one instance, the school choir appears annually in concert before the head of state.

Many sponsoring mission societies encourage graduate study during furlough, and some provide incentives toward that end. Faculty awareness of current trends and changes in curriculum needs improvement, but we commend these schools for their concern regarding in-service training and faculty workshops. In most cases adequate time was set aside for our consultantship visit; in some cases, faculty gave up part of vacation periods to attend.15

Currency in teaching practice is hindered, however, by outdated textbooks and exceedingly limited library holdings. Most schools have textbook editions dating from the early 1960's or earlier, before important revisions made literature anthologies and history books more useful teaching aids. Some schools are attempting to modernize their choice of textbooks but are finding it difficult to do so because of inordinate delays in shipping, obstruction by customs officers, or cost.

Similarly, librarians find themselves hampered in their efforts to improve their acquisitions. Particularly unfortunate is the delay in periodicals. Quite in contrast to

the American government-supported schools, whose newspapers
and magazines include current issues sent by air mail, few
mission schools have more than the current international
edition of *Time* or *Newsweek* (rarely both); fewer still
have yesterday's *Herald-Tribune*. In January, a school in
Japan had just received its September magazines; in April,
schools in Kenya and Ethiopia were displaying December issues. Remarkably few schools include among their periodicals national publications in English, although some receive the lavish propaganda magazines from the United
States Information Agency.

College-bound students are particularly hampered by a
lack of adequate library resources, especially in the ra-
pidly expanding literatures of contemporary culture, the
social sciences, and modern biography. Even in typical
areas of school library strength--the popular encyclo-
paedias, for example--these schools are often weak. In
preparing a paper on *Macbeth* (an assignment that extended
over our visit to four schools), our son Don found little
critical reading available; the extent of one school's
Shakespearean commentaries was a 1906 introduction to the
Complete Works.

But we must turn now to that aspect of curriculum which
we had supposed would most clearly set these schools apart
from the typical American school and serve to exemplify
Christian schooling at its most essential--namely, in their
teaching of the Bible. As Christian schools, each claims
in its literature to give importance to instruction in the
Word of God. In elementary schools, for the most part, we
find this claim maintained through daily Bible lessons,
memorization programs, and other visible attempts on the
part of many classroom teachers to coordinate various
elements of learning with lessons from the Bible.

In the secondary schools, unfortunately, the same cannot
always be said. To begin, courses designated for Bible
instruction rarely meet more than two class periods per
week. But Bible classes meet less than half as often. It
does not require much reasoning ability to discern that in
these schools Bible classes must be less important than
others.

Yet such is not the attitude of administrators. They do
not intend to diminish the significance of the Scriptures.

Instead their decision to schedule Bible class less frequently than others seems to be founded upon two assumptions from which we must demur.

The first assumption is that these teenagers already
possess sufficient Biblical knowledge because of their
upbringing in Christian homes; therefore, they can afford
a less vigorous regimen of study. We consider this attitude to be an instance of wishful thinking. It certainly
has never been borne out in our experience in Bible
classes, whether at Stony Brook or elsewhere, that students
from today's Christian homes have any more than a rudimen-
tary knowledge of the Bible.

The second assumption, derived from the first, is that
teenagers already so well informed about Christianity and
surfeited with the Scriptures will object to having further
studies imposed upon them. The self-contradictory nature
of this argument seems patent enough not to require further
comment.

Together these assumptions deprive Bible teaching of its
natural dignity and authority because from them flow a
series of consequences and indecision inimical to successful schooling. We observe the following to be true at most
secondary schools we visited:

1. *The Bible itself is rarely the primary text for study.*
Instead, students may read books *about* the Bible (*The Late
Great Planet Earth*), books on Christian behavior (*The
Taste of New Wine*), books about famous Christian athletes
(*The Goal and the Glory*).

A curious reasoning explains why the Bible is set aside,
especially in certain of the cooperatively sponsored
schools. Feeling that the study of the Bible is inextri-
cably tied to the development of controversial doctrines,
some schools attempt to avoid clashes among their consti-
tuents by minimizing the use of the Bible in the classroom.

In schools enrolling students from non-Christian families, the reason given for relegating the Bible to its
supplementary status is that these students, lacking the
presumed Biblical training of others from Christian homes,
would be placed at an unfair disadvantage. We counter by
stating that the open Bible on each student's desk is the

great leveler. The question facing each student ought not
to be, "How much do you already know?" but "How well can
you read the words-on-paper from the book in front of you?
How well can you comprehend what you read? How well can
you interpret and apply what you comprehend?"

Even where the Bible is the primary text, we rarely find
that the school has agreed on a version for classroom use.
While we encourage every student's freedom to choose which-
ever versions he wishes for personal study, the chaos we
find in classes without a standard text argues for adoption
of a single uniform classroom text.

2. *Schools appear to have no structure or continuity to the
teaching of Bible.* We have seen no syllabi, no materials
indicating course planning throughout the sequence of grade
levels, no evidence that schools have organized Bible
teaching in such a manner as to know which books are to be
taught in which courses to which age of students. Newly
arrived teachers seem to have total responsibility for organizing the content of their courses.

A scarcity of qualified teachers of Bible within such
circumstances complicates the problem. In the first place,
some administrators of Christian schools seem to feel that
any Christian teacher should be automatically capable (as
if by conversion experience) of teaching Bible. But the
Bible is a *book*--literature of the highest order, to be
sure, yet literature requiring a responsiveness to the
subtleties of language, metaphor, and rhetoric. Some
people, no matter how devout, lack this sensitivity to language and would not qualify as teachers in any kind of
reading course; much less do they qualify to teach the
Word of God, especially to an assumedly hostile class.

Secondly, most evangelical Christian colleges (including those whose graduates traditionally form the majority
of these teachers) now require fewer Bible credits than
were once necessary for a degree. Consequently missionary
teachers with credentials in biology or history or French
may not have enrolled in more than four or five quarter
courses in "Bible"; even all of these may not be in book
studies but in "Christ and Culture," archaeology, or church
history. Consequently, they may not know enough of the
Bible to teach it at all.

Even those teachers whose preparation has been in Biblical studies or who possess theological degrees may not
necessarily have learned the fine art of teaching the Bible
to adolescents.[16] We observe this anomaly of mission
society politics: When a man is thought to be ineffective
as a church planter or village evangelist, he is reap-
pointed to teach--often to teach Bible--in the mission
school.

Inexperience or the wrong kind of experience leads to
questionable teaching methods. Two examples will serve to
illustrate an all-too typical pattern of dubious methodology in Bible teaching.

At one school each 11th grade student was assigned "to
preach a 15-minute sermon based on the life of Christ."
The class, showing considerable understanding of the institution of preaching and its problems, protested against
the surreal conditions of the assignment. They pointed to
the inordinate difficulty for some in presentation, and
most important, the fraudulence for others, known disbe-
lievers, in preaching a sermon! The teacher, who had offered no prior instruction in homiletics, seemed shaken by
the intensity of the class's reaction against his assignment. "All I asked," he said innocently, "was for them to
preach a sermon. Why, they've been hearing sermons all
their lives!"

At a second school, a study of the life of Christ, for
9th graders, had proceeded to the end of the second term
with students unable to locate in the Scriptures incidents
as familiar as Nicodemus's visit or the conversion of the
woman at the well. Their instructor had adopted a wholly
eisegetical approach whereby the interview between Jesus
and the Syro-Phoenician woman (Matthew 15:21-28) was made
to stand against Ephesians 2:1-10. The result was that the
next classtime's quizzing revealed how little the students
knew about either passage, for neither had been studied in
context, in structure, or by any other valid principle of
hermeneutics.

As a result of these several conditions, we find many
teachers assigned to Bible classes discouraged, some even
unwilling to continue with their classes. One school re-
flects the general despair when its faculty petitions the
school board to permit a moratorium on all Bible teaching

until a committee on curriculum redesigns the program to
the faculty's satisfaction.

3. *The authority of the Scriptures as the inspired Word of
God is thereby undermined.* We recognize the seriousness of
this statement, for it can scarcely be uttered without
seeming to condemn; yet our purpose is not condemnation,
and the facts speak for themselves.

In schools where the Bible is taught less often and
sometimes less well than other subjects, including the
peripheral non-academic subjects, students are not slow to
perceive the minor scholastic importance accorded the
Bible. Especially is this true in schools that limit the
Bible teacher from assigning homework or that relegate
Bible to "pass/fail" grading while keeping per centage or
letter grades in other courses.

Lack of academic rigor in whatever subject always places
the teacher at a disadvantage. "If it's not worth working
hard for," reasons the teenager, "it's probably not worth
my time at all." The teacher thus finds himself apologizing for taking up the student's time, justifying the existence of the Bible course, arguing with students over Biblical tenets, sometimes without benefit of an unequivocal
institutional platform on which to stand.

No wonder a resulting climate of doubt pervades some of
these schools. For where Bible teaching is weakest, we observe, arguments over the unique Person of Jesus Christ,
the atonement and resurrection, and the very need for mission itself are at their highest. We believe a correlation
exists between adult slighting of the Scriptures and adolescent cynicism.

A concomitant problem arises when some schools feel per-
suaded to hire teachers whose religion is Hinduism, Islam,
or Buddhism--not to mention those few whose understanding
of Christian doctrine does not include a high view of
Scripture or, perhaps, the bodily resurrection of Jesus.
Toward this minority on the faculty, the administration
takes an attitude of tolerance automatically precluding
any strong emphasis upon the singularity of Biblical revelation and its call for faith in Jesus Christ.

4. *Development of an integration of Christian faith and learning, built upon an understanding that "in Christ are hid all the treasures of wisdom and of knowledge" (Colossians 2:3), is restricted by the absence of a strong Bible teaching program at the center of the curriculum.*

The combination of many factors accounts for this crippling weakness to Christian schools: Administration and faculty often untrained in the history and philosophy of Christian schooling; theologically and Biblically uninformed as to the significance of a Christian world-and-life view; uncommitted to the inherent relationship between what we believe and what we know; or even if willing to grant such a relationship, unsure as to the effective formulation of this integration.

Yet we find, in every school, a nucleus of concerned teachers and administrators aware of all these problems. This fact encourages us to feel that these schools are ready to reverse the unhappy course away from an anaemic program of Bible instruction. The very timing of our tour coincided, in several instances, with evaluative self-studies in which the school had reached similar judgments just prior to our visit. Nowhere is there opposition to reform in Bible teaching; indeed, correspondence received since completing our tour indicates that an invigorated attitude toward the teaching of Bible has begun to affect schools. What is now needed is a supporting program to assist mission schools and teachers in enlarging their sense of Bible teaching to include its comprehensiveness in the quest for wholeness of truth.

7

Worship, Evangelism and Service

Each elementary school begins, or schedules part of, the school day in worship, usually consisting of classroom prayers and Scripture reading and perhaps a song. On occasion, elementary classes throughout the school may meet for joint worship, as sometimes happened during our visits.

Secondary schools follow widely differing patterns. One school begins each day, at 6:55 a.m., with a 5-10 minute devotional, followed by 20-25 minutes of compulsory Bible memorization. At the opposite scale of intensity is the school whose occasional worship alternates with assembly programs, perhaps every six weeks or so. Some schools schedule a weekly period for worship, often 45-50 minutes long. Only two secondary schools hold daily chapel services of 15-20 minutes' duration.

Attendance at these meetings is required at all but one school, where an interesting reversal in responsibilities prevails. The school rejects what it sees as the role of bully in forcing worship upon reluctant students; but it supports the parents' right to insist on the child's attendance. In order to maintain that parental responsibility and to dramatize decision-making as a joint parent-child action, the school requires each family to specify whether or not high school students are committed to attending worship meetings. Then the school holds the student accountable for living by that commitment.

Some schools conduct Sunday worship in the campus chapel
or auditorium; others rely upon the services of local English-speaking congregations. In either case the Sunday
worship is likely to be adult-directed with as little student leadership as one might find in an evangelical church
in America. We would hope for efforts within these schools
at fostering greater student involvement in planning or
conducting public worship.

Sunday School, Pioneer Girls, Christian Service Brigade,
Awana Club, Young Life, Campus Life, and other youth groups
may meet on Sundays, often in the evening and sometimes as
a combined social hour. Leadership for these activities
may be drawn from the non-teaching staff, faculty wives, or
nearby parents; participants are usually the younger students.

Boarding schools hold evening devotions in the dormitories on a varying basis. At some, the meeting of dormitory residents is a business affair to discuss common problems and projects, concluded by prayer. Of course, the
manner of living together in a Christian school is a spiritual matter and as such rightly belongs to the forefront of
Christian concerns. At other schools, however, the purpose
of the dormitory meeting is understood to be entirely for
prayer and Bible study. Some schools hold these meetings
nightly, others weekly.

Likewise attendance expectations vary from school to
school. Only one of those schools holding nightly devotions requires nightly attendance; others require two or
three nights' attendance per week; still others make no
requirement at all. The same is true of schools holding
devotions less often.

In our experience these dormitory meetings can be most
useful in providing time for discussion of issues in small
groups. But we feel strongly that our most successful en-
counters have been with students who chose voluntarily to
attend. Under such circumstances we find students prepared to engage in serious discourse without further sti-
mulus than their own motivation.

On the contrary, we find little evidence of student-
initiated prayer meetings or Bible studies in schools where
evening devotions are a required appointment. With the

school insisting on group participation, student incentive
toward organizing their own devotions, public or private,
seems to be vitiated. "No one here would dare announce
that he was starting a prayer group," says an 11th grade
girl, "unless he's the most popular boy in the school.
There's too much expected of us already. We just don't
have time for any more meetings."

This girl's honesty reveals a problem created when administrative edicts smother student will. Teenagers in a
college preparatory school do have heavy calls upon their
time; students in a small school have that many more demands upon them, especially those who are natural leaders.
A school cannot reasonably expect even its more devout
Christian students to spend more time than they possess in
spiritual pursuits.

But the girl's remark also discloses conventional adolescent values and their relationship to a school's inner
spiritual growth. As we have said, whenever a Christian
school gives priority to student adherence to established
forms, that school reduces the importance of voluntary devotions. But more important, in the mind of the teenager,
the school preempts any need for imaginative innovation in
worship from the students.

Evangelism in a Christian school must be on-going in the
daily life and witness of each confessing Christian. But
it is also an administrative responsibility to incorporate
an evangelistic mission into the fabric of the school experience. Individually the believing teacher or student
may witness in the classroom, on the athletic field, in
the dormitory; but customarily the school will set aside
specific dates and times for announced periods of evangelistic emphasis.

I served as evangelistic speaker at several schools but
only one had so requested before our arrival; the other
evangelistic meetings developed rather in an *ad hoc* manner.
The school which had planned ahead was prepared in prayer
and had made suitable adjustments to its daily schedule to
make the 30-minute meetings convenient in time and location.
Of greatest interest to us was the fact that the school
also planned a weekend retreat for voluntary attendance by
those who had been motivated to respond during the previous
week's meetings. So, on Friday afternoon, some 65 students

in grades 9-12 hiked off to a campsite away from the school
campus to spend the remainder of the weekend in serious
Bible study and discussion of the Christian faith. Those
three days stand out in our memory as perhaps the most re-
warding of our tour.

We do not wish to congratulate organization for its own
sake, but it seems reasonable to argue for constructive
planning as a means of avoiding wasted time and, particularly, as a means of allowing the visiting speaker sufficient time in advance to prepare his messages thoughtfully
and specifically.

Students and teachers with whom we discussed evangelism
agree that most conversion commitments do not occur during
meetings in chapel or dormitory but in private interviews
with a teacher or other student or in solitude. Some
students, in fact, dispute the effectiveness of the
school's evangelistic week of meetings, holding that by
their very nature these meetings, from their first an-
nouncement, put antagonistic students on the defensive.
Whether or not this is so, the fact is that the Good News
preached with power by a new voice supported in prayer
often seems to encourage believers to augment their present
witness; from this encouragement new commitments are sure
to result.

But as every pastor knows, worship and evangelism in a
vacuum soon cease to satisfy. What is needed is faith-fol-
lowed-by-works. In the Christian school as in the church,
the problem for Christians is to find appropriate ways of
putting their faith into action, to find means of service.

Service in the school, as in the church, must begin at
home--within the family, the smallest social unit; in
boarding school terms, with the roommate and in the dormitory. Students (especially those from legalistic Funda-
mentalist backgrounds) need to be taught that courtesy and
kindness to others are at least as important as tithing;
that thoughtfulness, helpfulness, a pleasant attitude, a
willing spirit are all manifestations of service. It will
do no good, surely, to talk about service outside the dor-
motory and beyond the campus bounds if right relations do
not prevail within.

But to achieve this end, significant leadership must come from dormitory supervisers. Recommending projects, seeing them carried out, evaluating their results are responsibilities that devolve upon adult residents. A shared concern throughout the faculty is also important. Much of the eventual growth of students through service depends upon the examples they find among their teachers and dorm parents. Students rightly expect these service projects to be worthy; if they are "Mickey Mouse" or trivial, they will not command student respect and participation.

We have found whole dormitories devoted to gathering money, clothing, and food for famine victims; other students have resolved to go without certain foods--meat or desserts--at stipulated meals so that the cost of these foods might be contributed to others' needs. At these same schools we can point to services being rendered in the immediate community--a building being renovated to provide a work center for the elderly, a baby-sitting arrangement to enable mothers to attend Bible studies.

Some schools, however, appear to offer no chance for their students to serve the community, and these same schools are often the most restless and divided internally. Until this defect is corrected, the Christian school without service falls short of the standard established by the One who said, "Freely you have received; freely give."

8

Athletics

On the whole the schools we visited provide more than adequate programs for intramural and interscholastic competition in sports; some are truly excellent. Several schools boast national championship teams. The sports most widely offered are baseball, basketball, cross country, field hockey, soccer, swimming, tennis, track and field, volleyball, and wrestling. One school also fields five squads in rugby.

Coaching is earnest and remarkably skilled. Some schools benefit from the availability of short-term workers with excellent competitive experience--a former world's recordholder in the shot put, a former professional baseball player, a recent "Venture for Victory" basketball star. Other schools depend upon coaches who have developed their skills as students of the sport.

Each school recognizes the importance of competition as a fulfillment of disciplined practice and training. Even though budgets are limited, schools are willing to support the cost of team travel, which in some cases means flights to distant locations, even to other countries. Locally competition must sometimes be found with adult industrial or military teams. From our observation the teenaged schoolboys behave with poise and maturity, even in spite of sometimes less than sportsmanlike opposition.

Some schools combine athletic events with public relations for the school or mission society. The national community may be invited to attend home games. On a trip away from school, members of the team and accompanying faculty may participate in an evangelistic effort at the point of competition.

One or two schools regard participation in athletics as a privilege and use the threat of an athlete's suspension from competition to encourage better behavior, higher grades, or to enforce compulsory Scripture memorization.

Generally, however, we find a healthy attitude toward sports and competitiveness. At no school is the athletic program out of balance with the rest of the curriculum. At its best, athletics in these schools fulfill a dual role, providing present tests of courage and character that also train for the future.

We are particularly impressed by those intramural programs that provide competitive opportunities for boys and girls lacking interscholastic talents.

Several schools conduct physical education classes in addition to their full athletic schedule. At one school, instruction in track and field events made it possible for every student in secondary grades to learn the technique of various events; at the same time children in primary grades participated in the President's Youth Fitness Tests and received badges and certificates for their accomplishments.

Few schools include instruction in health education or first aid, although two or three schools involved in mountaineering or hiking programs prepare candidates before major outings with elementary first aid tips.

9

The School and Community

A school is a social organism, a congress of individuals
brought together because their purposes in work and study
coincide at one location, the school campus. But this ran-
dom assortment of children, adolescents, and adults does
not *de facto* constitute a *community* in any sense of the
word. *Community* is an ideal attained only after members of
the group have identified and given express priority to
elements of living that bind them together. At the same
time, individual members must agree to submerge some personal preferences in the interests of the larger whole.[17]

For the purposes of this brief report, we are citing
only three specific areas of school experience around which
to shape our observations. Our particular emphasis is upon
residential aspects: eating customs, boy-girl relationships,
and cross-cultural exposure. Obviously, other important
areas, such as worship and service, also call for a sense
of community. Readers are invited to infer this importance
from comments already made in this report.

1. *Eating customs*. The Christian Church has always placed
a strong emphasis upon the act of eating together. The New
Testament contains many references to communal eating--from
the institution of the Lord's Supper and injunctions concerning it to the revelation of consummate fellowship at
the marriage supper of the Lamb. But Scripture does not
reserve its blessing only for the ceremonial feasts of the

Church; even the eating of our daily bread, for which we
are instructed to pray and give thanks, is a sacramental
moment.

Perhaps it is a sorry reflection of the typical Christian home that few of these Christian schools hold their
meals in such reverence. Instead there is a hurried ten-
sion accelerated by various groups of students; in some
schools this excessive haste is unabated by adult control
because there is no adult present! Of the boarding schools
in which we were fed some or all our meals in the dining
hall, three follow the policy of excluding faculty from
eating with students; three others maintain a faculty table
apart so that students are seldom seated with adults.
Meals are gobbled down without apparent regard for nutri-
tion, digestion, or manners. In two schools it was not unusual for food throwing and other breaches of civility to
break out, including haughty and disparaging treatment of
the national waiters or kitchen crew. No one knows how
many instances there may be of bullying, hounding, hazing,
or other schoolboy cruelties to children perpetrated by
their peers during mealtimes.

Not surprisingly under such conditions, one no longer
hears public prayers of blessing and thankfulness before
meals at several of these Christian schools. Contrast-
ingly, in schools where adults are present at the table
with students and where grace is said, decorum fitting the
occasion is commonplace.

We go back to an earlier comment: Few administrators and
faculty in these schools have the experience to recognize
the peculiar nature of the boarding school and its particular call for an exemplary adult presence in most spheres of
daily experience. To be sure, every boarding school headmaster and teacher needs relief from constant association
with students; every headmaster and teacher anticipates the
stage of maturity when a select group of students can maintain an orderly dining room. But realistically speaking,
every adult knows what happens when 200 teenagers are left
alone without example or supervision three times a day at
meals.[18]

Yet one headmaster argues for never taking meals with
his students by saying, "We're a family"--by which he means
his wife, himself, and their children. They have invio-

lable rights of privacy. His school, however, refers to
itself as "a home away from home." These two claims,
therefore, are contradictory; administratively viewed, the
headmaster's "family" already envelopes all those placed
under his care, and presumably he is as responsible for
this larger "family" as for his natural family.

Here, then, is a phase of communal living in which
Christian values need to be reasserted. Apart from the
school's responsibility to maintain a wholesome environment
in which to eat, there is its patent Christian obligation
to obey the Word of God in offering thanks for food and
other gifts. But even beyond these fundamentals lies the
great opportunity for developing personal relationships
around the dinner table. At its highest, the mealtime may
become an interlude of fellowship in a true spirit of
Christian community, as it was for Cleopas and his compan-
ion at Emmaus, who told how the Risen Christ "had been recognized by them at the breaking of the bread" (Luke 24:
35).

2. *Boy-Girl Relationships.* In the natural order of things
adolescent boys and girls become attracted to each other,
some earlier and more passionately than others. They need
both an opportunity to develop whole and healthy relationships with the opposite sex and also mature guidance in
that development.

In a small school, relationships are limited by student
population; when that school is a North American enclave in
a foreign country, the limitations are even tighter, especially if the school is located at some distance from urban
centers. There are no boys or girls who live across the
city, who attend a different church or school, yet who
might become one's boy friend or girl friend. In other
words, there are seldom any acceptable alternatives to the
immediate choice of friends from within one's own school.
Romantic attachments with nationals are discouraged, if not
forbidden.

As a result, the fear of being excluded from the web of
social activities constrains many students to make firm relationships early in adolescence. Pairing of couples is
taken seriously. Students in these schools are still maintaining the custom of "going steady," with all its pre-
courting implications of singular devotion--a stage no

longer in vogue among teenagers in America. We see almost
no sign of group relationships such as are common in America—odd numbers of boys and girls enjoying each other's
companionship without necessarily staking claim to any
particular person.

Likewise, opportunities for growth socially may be
limited to a schedule of on-campus parties, which for all
their planning and earnest effort on the part of committees, cannot avoid the sameness of location and participants.

These are problems inherent in the size and isolation of
the school; but they might be minimized if adult attitudes
towards teenage relationships were more positive than is
sometimes the case. Adult guidance must be expressed in
positive terms. Adults must make plain their joy in a
teenager's commencing his rites of passage into adulthood
and responsibility. If instead negative standards are em-
phasized, a wall of suspicion and distrust soon rises between adults and students, and the natural order of boy-
girl relationships becomes twisted into a contest of wills:
the school dictating its list of prohibitions, students de-
vising means to circumvent them.

And circumvent them, they will! The proclamation of the
"six-inch rule" and the delegation of nightly teams of
faculty serving as "kissing patrols" to scour the campus
are no safeguard in themselves against undesirable effects
of teenaged urges. Only naivete fails to recognize that
youth thwarted in one direction will discover another,
sometimes more extreme. At one of the most strictly
governed schools, the headmaster confided that only a month
before a boy had contracted venereal disease in a brothel
in the nearby city.

Instead of pouncing upon signs of affection between
teenagers as though they were in themselves illegitimate,
Christian schools need to nurture and encourage healthy
relationships through strong Biblical teaching about the
dignity of persons, the holiness of the body, and the
sublimity of physical union as a metaphor for the union of
Christ and his Church. This kind of teaching must also be
accompanied by careful, responsible instruction in sex education ("family living," if that term is preferred). Our
discussions with students, particularly during devotions in

the older dormitories and especially among 11th and 12th
grade girls, reveal a disturbing lack of informed understanding of normal bodily development and functions. All
too often, we fear, strongly negative emphases upon boy-
girl relationships have been most common at schools without
any formal sex education.

But formal instruction of itself is not sufficient
either. "Example is the school of mankind," said Edmund
Burke, "and they will learn at no other." So husbands and
wives in a Christian school must also exemplify the best
characteristics of Christian marriage, including affection-
ate regard for one another. Along with whatever other
qualifications and credentials a teaching couple may present, the mission society ought to be able to recommend
these candidates to the school administration for evidences
of a warm and whole relationship with each other. In per-
fect candor, we must ask why mission boards and schools
permit obviously unhappy and incompatible couples to remain
in so sensitive a position as that of teachers in a Christian boarding school.

3. *Cross-cultural exposure.* Among the most apparent advantages that ought to accrue to students in overseas schools
is that of participating in elements of the culture around
them. Instead it appears that some schools often exclude
their students from contact with the national tradition
available to them. Their curriculum, their teachers (with
few exceptions), their dress, their sport and recreation,
their music and worship are all North American. They exist,
as it were, in isolation from the pulsating stream of life
with its customs, its costumes, its history, its current
affairs--its *people.*

Even as missiologists warn us against cultural superior-
ity in our presentation of the Gospel, so educators have
been warning us against a narrowly circumscribed curriculum.
One might suppose that courses of study in schools as
widely separated as Japan, India, and East Africa would re-
flect some of the distinctives of their national settings.
The fact is that all these schools might have been located
within the same county in Oregon or Pennsylvania, so similar are their course offerings. Only the fact that a
national language is taught in most (but not all) mission
schools sets them apart culturally from the typical neigh-
borhood American high school.

As in the classroom, so also in the chapel. Euro-
American forms of worship prevail exclusively, whether
these be the liturgy of a Lutheran order of service or the
informality of a Southern Baptist hymn sing. Not once were
we introduced to Asian or African indigenous modes of worship.

A major exception to these failures in cross-cultural
exposure is the food served in school dining rooms and in
the homes of faculty and other missionaries. Students
identify readily with national dishes--*tempura* in Japan,
chappatis in India, *injera wat* in Ethiopia--often express-
ing their preference for them over Western diet. They are
eager to know the visitor's tastes, happy when we concur
with their delight, scornful when we dare to make a face!

Could not some of the same adaptation to culture occur
elsewhere in the lives of these students? We know at
firsthand that they associate with nationals when they are
at home with their parents. Some of their playmates are
nationals; often their own fluency in the language exceeds
their parents' simply because they are well integrated with
the nationals at home. Why, then, do they leave this integration behind when they enter the mission school?

The mission school can be a primary training ground for
the next generation's missionaries. What an asset to any
missionary, to have been reared and educated in the culture
in which one is called to serve! To know the people, their
gestures, their needs, their mores, but even more: to know
what has formed their cultural heritage. Yet we find only
one school teaching even an elective course in national re-
ligions and philosophy--by the way, the most popular course
in that school; and no school with a program whereby students can enter into the life of the national community to
learn from its elders.

Unless the mission school cultivates an attitude of acceptance towards the people in whose country the school and
its system of education are alien, the school can never expect to be an effective working member in the mission enterprise. It will always be an appendage, a costly necessity if not a nuisance. It lies within the school's power
to develop learning resources out of local festivals, geo-
graphical and environmental landmarks, politics, publications, museums, art exhibitions, films, music, folk dancing,

and many other national qualities of life. These will not
only enrich the lives of students and faculty alike but
also demonstrate that the school is interested in being one
with the people--interested in participating in the pheno-
menon of *community*.

10

Conclusion and Recommendations

To advance the mission of world evangelization, the Church must be willing to recognize, more than it has in the past, the significance of family involvement in cross-cultural evangelism. A married missionary is not a simple integer; he has a wife and probably a family of several children.

"Before I was called to be a missionary," says one man with 18 years' experience in Africa, "I was called to be a husband and father. For me there is no higher calling."

The missionary family is a unit; yet because of various factors the family may find itself separated, the children attending school at some distance from home and their parents' place of service. This separation can be sustained, both by parents and children, without undue emotional or psychological distress, provided that
(1) both parents and children understand the reason for their separation and prepare adequately for its positive consequences;
(2) the school fulfills its purposes in providing a residential education that is whole and wholly Christian.

To achieve the first goal, parents must be able to feel and express confidence in the school to which they send their children. Thus the primary obligation rests upon the school as an institution and its sponsoring mission board to create this confidence.

Missionary parents have a right to expect that their
children will receive an education thoroughly grounded upon
a philosophy of knowledge that endeavors to "compel every
human thought to surrender in obedience to Christ" (2 Cor-
inthians 10:6)--in other words, a philosophy of education
that integrates faith and learning with action.

Such a philosophical grounding, articulated and put in
practice, does not happen merely by the founding of a
Christian school, administered by Christians. It must be
worked out; it must be incarnated in the lives of Christian teachers and students. It must be the daily concern
of every person connected with Christian schooling any-
where--that we, by example, teach our maturing students to
"think Christianly," as Harry Blamires expresses it.[19]

In order to "think Christianly," one must possess the
mind of Christ, in all its integrity and truth. The Christian mind must be manifest in the missionary convinced that
the Christian vocation of teaching is a valid calling from
God; that he has responded to this calling in obedience.
Likewise the mind of Christ demands that when a mission
society sponsors a school for missionary dependents, it
engages in its task with eagerness; not resigned, as it
were, to a fact of life, but seizing an opportunity to develop another generation responsive to the challenges of
overseas evangelism.

A few days before embarking on this tour, I met with the
faculty of the School of World Mission at Fuller Theological Seminary. During a wide-ranging conversation, which
touched on many areas whose importance I could only recognize in retrospect, one remark stood out vividly. The
elder statesman of world mission and church growth, Dr.
Donald McGavran, leaned out of his chair, shook his finger
at me, and said, "You tell those people who run mission
schools that they have an obligation to raise the standing
of missionary parents to *heroic* stature!"

We commend individuals and schools who are working together to achieve these high purposes. But we urge mission
organizations, school boards and administrators, missionary
faculty, and the evangelical members of the Body of Christ
to consider the following recommendations.

We recommend that

(1) each sponsoring mission society, in conjunction with its school authorities, write and begin to implement a stated philosophy of Christian schooling, along with goals and objectives in curriculum; at the same time they must be aware that education is a human process in constantly changing states that can never be frozen into a static methodology;

(2) as much as possible, administrators become familiar with the practices of other Christian schools, through study, inter-school visits, and conferences;

(3) organizations of overseas Christian schools begin sharing information through a central agency;

(4) study programs or workshops for teachers (present and prospective) be established at one of the centers for the study of world mission;

(5) mission societies be more aggressive in publicizing the need and work of their missionary dependents' schools;

(6) the teaching of the Bible be given a new priority and that careful study of instruction goals and methods be undertaken;

(7) other aspects of curriculum be carefully reexamined to eliminate a parochial American education and replace it with a truly international education;

(8) greater opportunities for student responsibility be found in the development of self-government and discipline for behavior and study;

(9) fuller awareness on the part of administration and faculty be shown of the adolescent's need for self-expression, especially in terms of spiritual questions, doubt, or disbelief, without fear of the loss of personal dignity and respect;

(10) new patterns of worship, evangelism, and service, including indigenous approaches, be explored and that students be more fully included in the planning of such programs;

(11) a more enlightened attitude toward all aspects of the school-as-community be adopted, including the making of necessary adjustments to provide for more integral relationships among persons.

Throughout this report we have concentrated on the opinions and judgments of mission society executives, school administrators and faculty, residence supervisors, parents, visiting observers--all adults. A final recommendation might be that, in future, a greater sensitivity be shown to the attitudes of the children themselves. After all, they are the ones for whom these schools are being maintained.

At Bingham Academy, Addis Ababa, Ethiopia, students in ninth and tenth grade English classes wrote poems to express their sense of what it means to be members of missionary families. Two of these poems seem particularly worth noting.

Living behind the times,
Yet above the times,
Always having an escape route from persecution;
Never having a way to be away from it all.
Enjoying life, only seeing a part of it,
That's being an M. K.
Confusion and Understanding mingled.
Knowing less about life,
But experiencing more.

                                        Audrey Martin
                                        Age 15, Grade 10

Going to a boarding school
Adopting many Moms and Dads from the staff
A close-knit dorm family
Sharing a bedroom with nine girls

An exciting life
Travel--by jet, DC-3, boat, bus, Land Rover, motorcycle,
            mule, horescart,
Living between two cultures
Being grateful when you see others' great needs

Wearing hand-me-downs
Using electrical appliances only three hours each night
Not being able to use all recipes in the cookbook because
              you don't have the right ingredients
Living in a mud home with warped floors and a tin roof

Feeling "out of it" when you go back home
Hardly knowing some close relatives at all
Going to a different church every Sunday on furlough
Meeting crowds of new people

Being treated royally by humble nationals
Seeing first-hand the effects of the Gospel on heathen
              lives
Wondering how long the present government will last--and
              where you'll be after that

Ruth Dye
Age 14, Grade 9

Notes

[1]Although few evaluations of mission-sponsored schools
have been conducted, at least four have received accredita-
tion from the Middle States Association of Colleges and
Secondary Schools: Woodstock School, Kodaikanal School,
Rift Valley Academy, and Faith Academy. There is as yet no
comprehensive report, however, on the quality or distin-
guishing features of the education offered by these
schools.

[2]Frank E. Gaebelein, *Christian Education in a Democracy*,
New York, 1951.

_____, *The Pattern of God's Truth*, New York,
1954.

D. Bruce Lockerbie, *The Way They Should Go*, New York, 1972.

[3]Stephen Neill, et al., *Concise Dictionary of Christian
World Mission*, London, 1970, p. 551. The entry, headed
"Short Term Missionaries" (contributed by Donald P.
Smith, Personnel Secretary, Commission on Ecumenical Mission and Relations, United Presbyterian Church in the USA)
optimistically declares, "Later many enter long-term service." Our observation concerning short-term appointees
among teachers and dormitory personnel would revise down-
wards, from "many" to "few."

[4]The May 1974 issue of *Overseas Information Service Bulletin,* published by Inter-Varsity Fellowship, 39 Bedford Square, London, England, provides nine legal-sized pages of listings for short-term appointments in Christian vocation. Several openings are indicated in schools for missionary children, including a request from Overseas Missionary Fellowship for "Houseparents/'Dorm aunties' for supervision of children in boarding schools."

[5]Ralph E. Bressler, "MK Education: What's the Score?" and "MK Education: What Is the Purpose?" *The Alliance Witness,* November 7, 1973 and January 16, 1974.

[6]Conversation with the Reverend Robert Alter, Superintendent, Woodstock School, February 21, 1974.

[7]"Objectives and Philosophy," *Kodaikanal School Project Design,* January 1974, p. 2.

[8]See Neill, *Concise Dictionary of Christian World Mission.* While one does not expect an admittedly "concise" work to touch on every topic possible, we are disappointed not to find in this otherwise admirable volume any treatment whatsoever of missionary dependents' education.

[9]I am particularly indebted to Dr. Floyd Travis, Superintendent of the American Community School, Addis Ababa, Ethiopia, for his courtesy and hospitality during my visit to his school.

[10]On a lecture tour of a dozen Christian colleges, taken in November 1973, just prior to this tour, I met and talked with numbers of college students who are graduates of these and other missionary schools. They voiced varying degrees of negative feeling--from dismay to outrage to contempt--at the manner in which the North American churches supporting their parents treat them as "MKs."

[11]The exceptions to this latter attitude are children born abroad who have spent, perhaps, not more than two widely separated years in the United States or Canada. For them, *home* is the Asian or African country in which their parents serve; its customs and dress, as well as its language, are theirs. America is foreign.

[12]*Inequality: A Reassessment of the Effect of Family and Schooling in America,* New York, 1972.

[13]Although most of these secondary schools participate in the College Entrance Examination Board's Scholastic Aptitude Test (SAT) and Achievement Tests (ACH), none has the Advanced Placement Program. This program, now twenty years old, qualifies secondary school candidates to validate work done in school for college credit. In several instances, the school testing counselor knew little or nothing about the AP Program.

[14]See pages 50-51.

[15]During the summer of 1973, Azusa Pacific College, Azusa, California, sent a team of four faculty members to South America to work with teachers in mission schools. Called "Operation Impact," this program consisted of a two-week conference for teachers, held at Lomalinda, Colombia. Three one-week conferences followed in Brazil, Bolivia, and Ecuador. In all, the program reached some 100 teachers from 17 schools in eight countries. Participants were Dr. Leo T. Phearman, Dr. John Carlson, and Dr. Larry Birch, all of the Department of Education, and Mr. Ron Cline, Dean of Students, at Azusa Pacific College.

At this writing I have not read a report of their program which is intended to continue through the summer of 1975.

[16]The grand failure of Christian higher education, and especially of those colleges purporting to be leaders in "Christian education," is the failure to prepare *teachers of the written Word.* Nowhere is this lapse more apparent than in the experience of would-be Bible teachers in Christian schools, trained in Vacation Bible School methods, but incapable of handling the language and literature that is "the Word of truth."

We are encouraged to learn that Geneva College, Beaver Falls, Pa., plans to institute a course of study leading to certification in elementary or secondary education for teachers intending to serve in Christian schools. According to the prospectus, candidates for the degree will augment their regular program of studies with courses in Bible and theology.

[17]Our son Don has written a definition of *community* in a
report submitted as part of his schoolwork to The Stony
Brook School: "In a boarding school, where different styles
and backgrounds collect, the unifying factor should be the
development of co-operation through which unpractised ha-
bits become natural, where conflicting ideas can exist
without causing a divorce in the school; in other words, a
community. And in the dorm a community operates, not a
'family,' because no one is ever from the *same* background.
And so a dorm striving for a family relationship can only
go so far, whereas in a community we must compromise our
differences by submerging some of them, while also holding
onto others, thereby drawing everyone out in their own
ways."

[18]Economic restrictions bind some teachers from eating with
students. Schools that now impose meal charges on personnel who eat in the dining hall discourage faculty who find
it less expensive to hire a national cook to prepare their
meals at home. In our opinion, when budgeting systems
stand in the way of an essential good, such systems should
be changed.

[19]*The Christian Mind,* London, 1966.

About
the Author . . .

Since 1957, D. Bruce Lockerbie has taught English and Bible at The Stony Brook School, a Christian secondary school on Long Island.   In 1974, he and his wife Lory, accompanied by their teenaged children, served as consultants to Christian schools in Asia and Africa.   This book is his report of their findings.

Among Lockerbie's other publications are *The Way They Should Go* (Oxford University Press), *The Liberating Word: Art and the Mystery of the Gospel* (Eerdmans), and a dozen textbooks on composition and literature.   He is a frequent contributor to *The New York Times Book Review* and other periodicals.

DATE DUE

MAR 27 '85			
F			
NOV 27 '85			

DEMCO 38-297

Other Books by the William Carey Library

General

Church Growth and Group Conversion by Donald A. McGavran $2.45p

The Evangelical Response to Bangkok edited by Ralph D. Winter $1.95p

Growth and Life in the Local Church by H. Boone Porter $2.95p

Message and Mission: the Communication of the Christian Faith by Eugene Nida $3.95p

Reaching the Unreached: A Preliminary Strategy for World Evangelization by Edward Pentecost $5.95p

Verdict Theology in Mission Theory by Alan Tippett $4.95p

Area and Case Studies

Aspects of Pacific Ethnohistory by Alan R. Tippett $3.95p

The Baha'i Faith: Its History and Teachings by William Miller $8.95p

A Century of Growth: the Kachin Baptist Church of Burma by Herman Tegenfeldt $9.95c

Church Growth in Japan by Tetsunao Yamamori $4.95p

A New Day in Madras by Amirtharaj Nelson $7.95p

People Movements in the Punjab by Margaret and Frederick Stock $8.95p

The Protestant Movement in Italy by Roger Hedlund $3.95p

Protestants in Modern Spain: the Struggle for Religious Pluralism by Dale G. Vought $3.45p

The Religious Dimension in Hispanic Los Angeles: A Protestant Case Study by Clifton Holland $9.95p

Taiwan: Mainline Versus Independent Church Growth by Allen J. Swanson $3.95p

Understanding Latin Americans by Eugene Nida $3.95p

Theological Education by Extension

Designing a Theological Education by Extension Program by Leslie D. Hill $2.95p

An Extension Seminary Primer by Ralph Covell and Peter Wagner $2.45p

The World Directory of Theological Education by Extension by Wayne Weld $5.95p

Textbooks and Practical Helps

Becoming Bilingual: A Guide to Language Learning by Donald Larson and William A. Smalley $5.95xp

God's Word in Man's Language by Eugene Nida $2.95p

An Inductive Study to the Book of Jeremiah by F.R. Kinsler $4.95p

Bibliography for Cross-Cultural Workers by Tippett $3.95p $5.95c

Principles of Church Growth by Weld and McGavran $4.95xp

Manual of Articulatory Phonetics by William A. Smalley $4.95xp

The Means of World Evangelization: Missiological Education at the Fuller School of World Mission edited by Alvin Martin $9.95p

Readings in Missionary Anthropology edited by William Smalley $4.95xp

377.6
L815

65936

new titles from...

William Carey Library

533 HERMOSA STREET • SOUTH PASADENA, CALIF. 91030

A CENTURY OF GROWTH: THE KACHIN BAPTIST CHURCH OF BURMA

Herman Tegenfeldt

Not simply a historical narrative, this contains anthropological, political, and leadership factors which had a part in the development of a church of more than 50,000 members. 500+ pages with 50+ photos, and 70 tables, maps, charts, and graphs.

$9.95

THE BAHA'I FAITH: ITS HISTORY AND TEACHINGS

William McElwee Miller

Miller has made a comprehensive study examining the origin, major tenets, attractions, and movement West and East of the Baha'i faith. The book contains a translation of the Holy Scriptures of the Baha'i faith, as well as excerpts from the author's correspondence with the late Jelal Azal, grandson of Subh-i-Azal and the Bab's immediate successor. A must for anyone seriously interested in the Baha'i religion. It has been called the first standard book on the subject.

$8.95

PRINCIPLES OF CHURCH GROWTH

Wayne Weld and Donald McGavran

Church leaders everywhere have long awaited the arrival of this improved and completely rewritten second edition. Initially written in Spanish, the demand was so great that it was translated into English in a preliminary edition. The book was originally prepared from writings and conferences by Donald McGavran.

$4.95X

THE MEANS OF WORLD EVANGELIZATION: MISSIOLOGICAL EDUCATION AT THE FULLER SCHOOL OF WORLD MISSION

edited by Alvin Martin

An academic manual of over 500 pages, this significant book is designed to give a full description of the 1972-74 missiology curriculum of the School of World Mission and Institute of Church Growth in Pasadena, California. Includes:

- areas of study constituting missiology

- missiological literature including abstracts of theses and dissertations

- guidelines for research and much more.

$9.95